Belle's Wish

WRITTEN BY
Lea Girsh

Belle's Wish

Published by Dr. Girsh Publishing

ISBN: 979-8-218-20305-4

Published in the United States of America

This book is dedicated to:

My beautiful EBB, my forever #1—Thank you for
making me a mother. You bring happiness and light to
my life. I love you beyond the shamayim.

My wonderful parents—Thank you for giving
me courage and strength to pursue my dreams.
I love you beyond words.

All the children in this world—keep your chin up,
know your worth, and believe in the power of acceptance,
support, and resiliency in overcoming challenges.

It was a bright, warm day, and Belle and her friends were playing in the school yard playground. While Belle was swinging on the swings, she overheard Lilly talking to Julie. "You know, my mom says she will be just fine on her own," Lilly shared.

As Belle watched tears fall down Lilly's face, a big feeling of sadness came over her. She felt sad for her friend.

Belle decided to leave the playground and walk home. But, as she did, tears fell from her eyes and rolled down her face.

She wished that her family would stay the same and that her parents would not separate. She wished that her daddy still lived in the same home. She wished that holidays stayed the same with both her mother and father in the home. She wished that she did not have to try to get used to this strange feeling inside of her belly. She also wanted to feel that she still belonged in a home with her Mama and Papa living together.

While she walked down the path leading to her house, Belle quickly wiped her tears and pretended to be alright because she did not want Mama to notice her sadness.

Pulling out her house keys, Belle unlocked the door and went in, looking at all the family pictures that hung on the wall in the entryway. Staring at the picture of Mama, Papa, and her smiling and holding hands at the playground, Belle wished they could have that moment back.

Just then, Mama walked into the hallway. "Hi, sweetheart. How was your day?"

"Good, Mama," Belle replied.

"Why don't you wash your hands and come eat with me, honey?"

Belle put her face down, swallowed her frown, and did as her Mama had asked.

After washing her hands, Belle sat down for dinner.

Oh, how she yearned for Papa to be at the dinner table—for them to be a happy family once again as they were before.

One of their family traditions was for everyone to go around the table and share their favorite parts of the day.

Mama began. "Okay, Belle, what was your favorite part of the day?"

"Coming home to you, Mama," Belle answered.

Something told Mama that Belle was not sharing her true feelings. "Sweetheart, it's okay to share anything you would like with me. Let's try another question: if you could change one thing about your day, what would that be?"

When Belle still hesitated, Mama added, "There are no right or wrong answers as long as you share what is in your heart, my dear."

Belle thought about the question for a while. She moved the broccoli bites and noodles around on her plate, searching for an answer. Mama listened silently. "Well, Mama, I wish we could be a happy family like that picture of the three of us on the playground."

"Belle," Mama said, "I am so proud of you. As difficult as this answer is for you and as much sadness as you have in your voice, you are choosing to hold on to something very special—a happy memory. Nobody will ever be able to take that away from you. Nobody will ever be able to erase your happiness, Belle."

"What do you mean, 'erase my happiness,' Mama?" Belle asked.

"Everyone has different memories and times that leave them feeling happy and content, like how you feel while you are at your favorite playground or while you are playing with your very best friend. No matter what anyone else says during those moments, you are happy and satisfied."

"Do you mean like when I get a good grade and you tell me how proud you are of me?"

"Exactly, my dear," Mama replied, smiling.

"Belle you see, when you have moments and times that leave you with a smile on your face, keep them close to your heart and know how blessed you are to be able to keep them there. Nobody can ever take them from you."

As they entered the living room and snuggled near each other, Mama rubbed Belle's back and explained, "Changes in life are hard. We don't like to do things differently because we are not used to them. If I asked you to start coming home and completing your homework before eating a snack, when all along you were used to first having a snack after school, that would be strange for you, wouldn't it? Because you wouldn't be used to it."

"Yes, Mama. It would be strange."

"However, if we made it a habit to first do your homework and then have a snack because then you would have more time to get ready for dance class and your homework would be done, after a while you would be used to it—"

"But what does this have to do with Papa living here?" Belle interrupted.

"Well, when Papa lived here, you were used to seeing him every day... that was an important part of your day. So, it will take some time for us to get used to him not being here, but that does not mean you can't continue to keep him close to your heart.

If you want to talk to Papa, you certainly can. Just because important things that fit into our lives change, doesn't mean we have to stop valuing them or let them go away from us."

"So you mean that if Papa was important to me before, he can continue to stay important to me?" Belle asked.

"Of course, my dear. Your Papa loves you and will stay important to you forever," Mama said, smiling gently. "The people who matter most to us can remain in our lives, even if we don't see them as much. Not only can you call your Papa and speak with him, you can also write letters and plan special times to see him. Your relationship with your Papa is very special and it always, always will be."

"Mama, that makes a lot of sense to me. You always find a way to make me feel better."

"Well, Belle, how about we plan what you will do with your happy memories?"

Belle looked bewildered. "Mama, I am not sure what I can do with my happy memories. Do you think papa has happy memories of the three of us?" she asked.

"I certainly believe he does and I do have an idea of what you can do with both your questions and your thoughts," Mama responded. "When we write down our thoughts and our feelings, it is a good way for us to remember them and keep them. It also opens up more space in our minds to make other good memories and have other positive thoughts and feelings. This kind of writing is called 'journaling.'"

"So if I write down my questions, my thoughts, and my feelings, then I will never forget them and I can look at what I wrote anytime I want?" asked Belle.

"Yes, Belle, and you can also even write your thoughts and feelings in a letter and then decide if you want to share them with anyone else," Mama explained.

"Thank you, Mama, that is a great idea. You think Papa will like if I write him a letter?"

"I think he will love it. It is getting late my dear, so why don't you go take a bath and brush your teeth and then we can do something special together before bed."

After Belle did what she had been asked to do, Mama knocked on her bedroom door. "I have something special for you Belle," she said, presenting her with a book that had the words "Belle's Wish" written on the cover in beautiful shiny red ink.

"Here is a new journal just for you, honey. Spend some time writing down your wishes, your thoughts, and your feelings. Think of it as your personal writing space," added Mama.

"Thank you so much Mama, can I start writing in it now? asked Belle, excited.

"Yes," Mama replied, smiling.

Opening the journal, Belle found a beautiful letter from Mama.

My dearest Belle,

Sometimes in life there are situations that happen which we cannot predict or may not be expecting. Some of these situations may be pleasant and some may be sad.

I like to think of it as "life happens." Life may not be easy at times, but that does not mean we are not strong enough, or don't have the power to handle them.

One very important message that I would like for you to always remember is that people cannot control how they feel. People can feel happy, sad, mad, glad, and many other feelings. People are allowed to feel how they feel. What really matters is what someone does with their feelings.

For example, just because someone is angry does not mean they have to scream or throw things, and just because someone is happy does not mean they have to flaunt it. We should always try to think carefully about what we do with our feelings when we experience them.

Making wise choices about how to cope with our feelings will allow us to live our best life possible.

So, my dearest Belle, you may be wondering how all of this applies to you. When you think about your Papa no longer living with us, or when you find yourself missing someone else in your life, you may find yourself feeling sad. Those feelings are normal. Even if you cry, my sweetheart, that is okay, because those are your feelings; those tears will not roll down your face forever.

You can choose to express your sadness by writing a letter to that person or you can write about your feelings in your journal. You can also take a walk with me or tell your best friend. You can think of your favorite song or even make a list of your favorite memories. It is important to acknowledge how you feel and not run from your feelings. When you believe that they are your feelings and that you own them, then you are prepared to handle your feelings better.

It is important to remember that once you let someone into your heart and you love them, you can always keep them safe there in your heart. Even if you don't see them as often as you would like, they can still fill your heart with warm memories. You can remember lessons they taught you and you can make a list, an album, or a collage of your favorite memories with them.

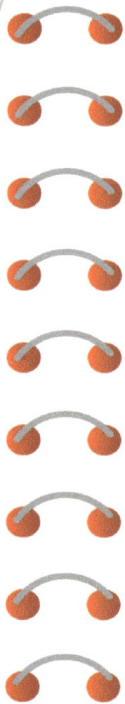

So Belle, life will happen and you won't always have what you want in your life, but never let go of your favorite memories and the special people that will live in your heart. My daughter, no matter where I am or where you are, you will always live in my heart.

With utmost love and magical wishes,

Mama

Belle felt so comforted by her mother's letter to her. Then, finding her favorite pen, she began journaling a letter to Papa.

When her mother returned to her bedroom,
Belle said, "Now I can tell you my favorite part of my
day..."

"What is it, Belle?"

Belle looked up at Mama and said, "Knowing that
no matter how I feel or what I think, I can share my
feelings and thoughts with you."

"You sure can, my dear daughter."

Mama squeezed Belle tight and kissed her forehead
before turning off the light and whispering,
"Goodnight..."

www.ingramcontent.com/pod-product-compliance
Lightning Source LLC
Chambersburg PA
CBHW040847300326
41935CB00035B/41